Seven
Skies
All
at
Once

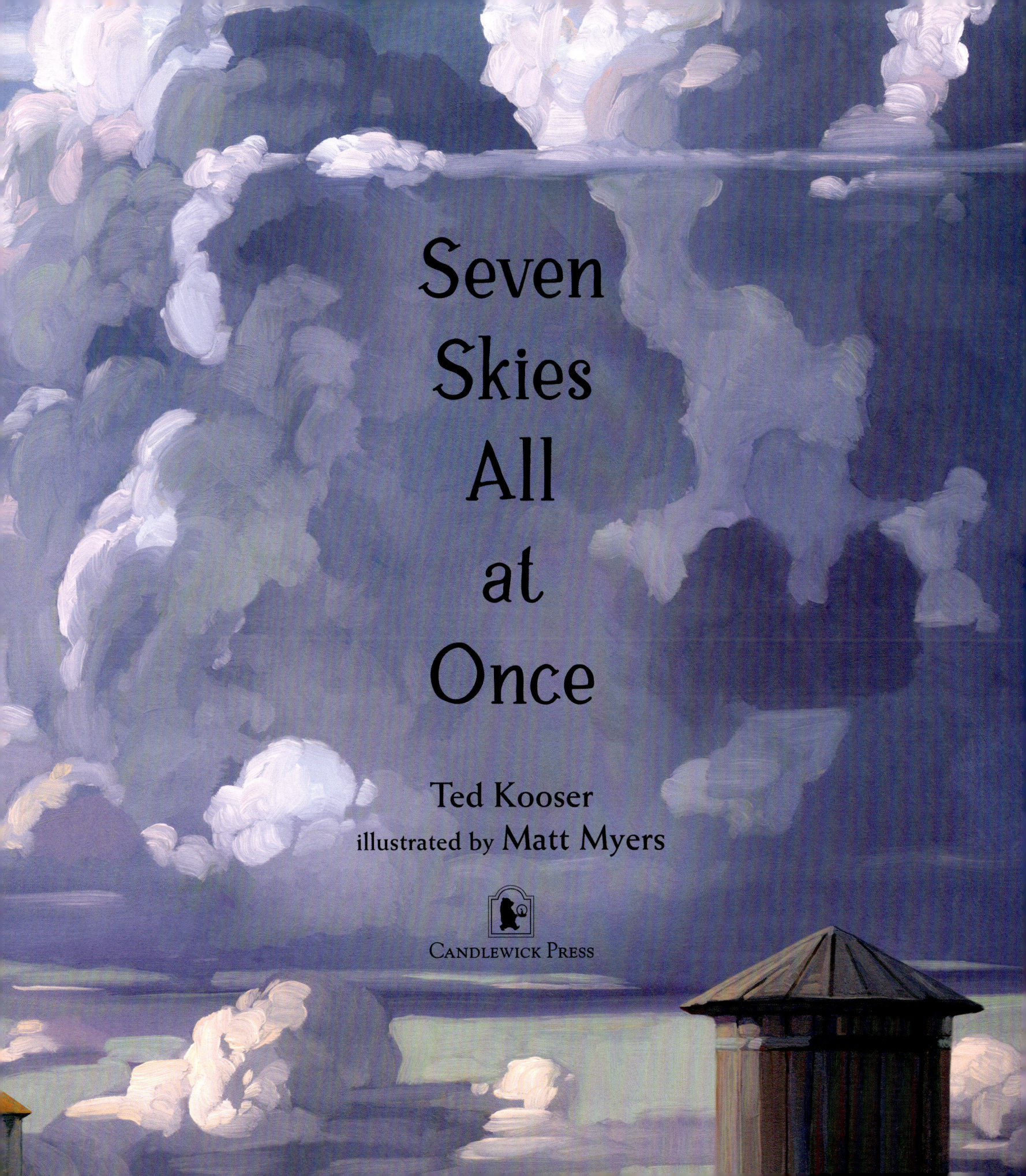

Seven
Skies
All
at
Once

Ted Kooser

illustrated by **Matt Myers**

CANDLEWICK PRESS

The skies had hung out their freshly washed clouds
to dry, wanting them to smell like air,
but it looked like rain might be coming.

So while one sky was unpinning its damp sheets
of cirrus from a frayed airplane contrail
strung from one end of the heavens
all the way to the other . . .

another sky hurriedly wadded up socks, T-shirts,
and underpants of cirrocumulus and stuffed them
into a basket woven of sunbeams.

In a reflection on a glass skyscraper, a third sky was carrying away great armloads of altocumulus . . .

and seen through a crack between two
tall buildings, a fourth sky, with big
muscly arms tattooed all over with all
kinds of birds, bustled past, carrying
pillowcases with fancy lace borders.

And then a fifth sky went past, wearing an apron piled high with cumulus, which it probably had taken down from some other contrail hidden behind one of the towers, perhaps strung between two of them.

Five skies, all with clouds, all taking them someplace
far over the horizon to stuff in a dryer to dry.

Then a sixth sky appeared,
dragging a heavy drop cloth of stratocumulus,
splattered all over . . .

the kind somebody painting the wall of the distance
would spread over a carpet of fields. And then . . .

all of a sudden a seventh sky approached at a run,
dragging a moth-eaten, dirty gray woolen blanket
of stratus with little pulses of white light within it . . .

and the wind began blowing,
and everything rattled . . .

and a huge cumulonimbus plumped down
on the city, squeezing the light out, so that
everything grew very dark, and then . . .

drop after drop, it finally started to rain,
and rained softly, then harder and harder.

And after it stopped, the skies left behind a green laundry basket with a handle that looked like a rainbow.

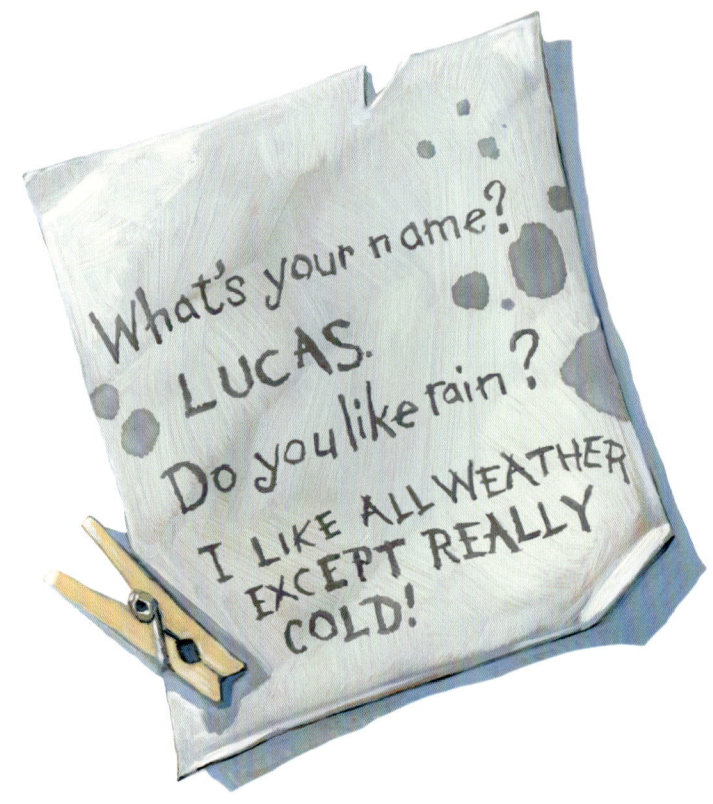

For Rose and Luke Gruntorad, our godchildren
TK

To Aaron and our long-distance friendship
MM

Text copyright © 2025 by Ted Kooser. Illustrations copyright © 2025 by Matt Myers. All rights reserved. No part of this book may be reproduced, transmitted, or stored in an information retrieval system in any form or by any means, graphic, electronic, or mechanical, including photocopying, taping, and recording, without prior written permission from the publisher. First edition 2025. Library of Congress Catalog Card Number pending. ISBN 978-1-5362-2900-4. This book was typeset in Weiss. The illustrations were done in oil on wood panel. Candlewick Press, 99 Dover Street, Somerville, Massachusetts 02144. www.candlewick.com. EU Authorized Representative: HackettFlynn Ltd., 36 Cloch Choirneal, Balrothery, Co. Dublin, K32 C942, Ireland. EU@walkerpublishinggroup.com.
Printed in Shenzhen, Guangdong, China. 25 26 27 28 29 30 CCP 10 9 8 7 6 5 4 3 2 1